30 Easy Vegan Christmas Recipes

To Enjoy Over The Festive Season

By Anita Thomas

Christmas is a time for celebration and when the holiday season is fast approaching, it's essential that your pantry is well stocked up so that you can easily enjoy making meals that all of the family will love.

Festive food usually involves turkey and all the trimmings, but for vegans and vegetarians who actively avoid all meats and animal products it can be a nightmare when visiting friends and relative's houses.

While veganism is on the rise, many people are still unaware of many of the tasty foods that are available to those who want to avoid meat products. It is sad in this day and age that some people may still believe that vegans are confined to eating lettuce and lentils when this couldn't be further from the truth.

Modern vegan meals offer an abundance of choice and are equally if not more nutritious than their meaty counterparts. Vegan Christmas meals in particular offer a plethora of menu options; everything from mouth watering appetisers like falafel can be made festive thanks to the addition of cranberries. Meanwhile mushrooms can even be made the main course when combined with chestnuts and cranberries to form delicious tarts.

My aim in putting this collection of recipes together was to show you how easy it is to make tasty vegan Christmas dinners that will wet the appetite of even the most ardent carnivore. There are thousands of reasons to adopt a plant-based diet, from animal rights to environmental reasons…but perhaps the biggest one for many is undoubtedly their health.

Avoiding animal products has become popular because meats, eggs and dairy products contain high levels of saturated fats and cholesterol, and as well as being harder to digest within the body, increase the risks of certain heart and cardiovascular diseases.

Adopting a plant-based diet is not as daunting as it may at first sound however. Many meals can be veganized or alternate dishes made to recreate the taste and flavors that you associate with some of your favorite festive meals.

I hope this book gives you some tasty inspiration to not only make these foods, but to also create your own meals from scratch using very basic and natural ingredients. Whether you're currently vegan or looking to make the switch, this book could give you the ammunition you need to persuade not only yourself and others that a plant based diet is the way to go. Enjoy!

Wishing you a green and festive Christmas,

Anita Thomas

Contents

Appetizers and Drinks

Cucumber Crackers with Hummus

This combination of cucumbers and hummus goes perfectly together, the flavors complimenting one another well.

Ingredients

1 cucumber
1 pot of hummus
A selection of wholegrain crackers
Sea salt and pepper for seasoning

Method:

1. Slice the cucumber width ways into discs.
2. Take the hummus of your choice and spread evenly over the crackers.
3. Place the cucumber slices on top and arrange on a platter. Enjoy!

Sweet and Spicy Maple Pecans

These taste delicious on their own as a snack and make a beautiful festive gift when placed in a bag and tied with a ribbon.

Ingredients

2 cups of pecan halves
1 teaspoon of pumpkin pie spice
1 teaspoon chili powder
3 tablespoons maple syrup
1 tablespoon extra virgin olive oil
1 teaspoon sea salt

Method:

1. Preheat the oven to 350 degree F, and then line a sheet pan with a piece of parchment paper.

2. Place the pecans into the prepared pan and sprinkle with the pumpkin pie spice, sea salt and chili powder.

3. Add the maple syrup and olive oil over the pecans by drizzling over the top. Stir the mixture well so that it's well combined and coats the nuts completely.

4. Bake in the oven for 15 minutes, ensuring that you stir every 5 minutes so that the nuts are redistributed. Place in the oven for a few more minutes so that the nuts obtain a deep golden brown color. Stir the mixture once more so that the nuts are evenly spread and allowed to cool in the pan. Then store in an airtight container until needed.

Marinated Olives

These make for a great starter before the main Christmas meal and are both tasty and nutritious, being high in Omega 3 and 6 essential fatty acids.

Ingredients:

2 6oz. cans of whole black or green olives, drained
½ cup of olive oil
4 garlic cloves, minced
¼ cup of fresh basil, chopped
2 tablespoons of balsamic vinegar
1 teaspoon of red pepper flakes
½ teaspoon of sea salt

Method:

1. Combine all of the ingredients together and mix together well within a covered dish.

2. Place within the refrigerator and then leave for 2 hours. Serve and enjoy!

Cranberry and Chestnut Falafel

This festive version of the traditional Moroccan recipe is an absolute delight when served with a creamy 'yogurt' like dip before the main course.

Ingredients

1 sweet potato, peeled and cut into chunks
200g of vacuum packed and ready cooked chestnuts
400g can of chickpeas, drained
1 serving of egg replacer such as Orgran No Egg or Ener-G Egg Replacer
85g cranberries, defrosted if frozen
4 tablespoons of vegetable or sunflower oil
2 teaspoons of chilli flakes
2 teaspoons of cumin seeds
1 garlic clove
A small pack of coriander, roughly chopped, plus more for serving
150g pot of soy yoghurt (for serving – optional)

Method:

1. Into a microwave-proof bowl, add the sweet potato and 1 teaspoon of water and cook on a high temperature for 2 mins. Then mash within a large bowl.
2. Place the chickpeas and the chestnuts into the food processor and pulse blend until the mixture is chopped well, but not pasty. Add the sweet potato, egg replacer, garlic, coriander and spices, then season and mix well using your hands.
3. Add in the cranberries to the mixture and shape into around 20 or so dessert sized balls.

4. Into a large non-stick frying pan, heat 2 tablespoons of oil and fry half of the falafel until golden, which should take about 2 minutes on each side.
5. Lift the falafel onto kitchen paper and then drain, repeating this with the second batch of falafel. Leave the falafel to cool for a few minutes and then serve with the soy yogurt and some coriander.

If necessary the falafel can be made 2 days ahead of time and then chilled for up to 3 days.

Vegan Eggnog

Relax and enjoy this delicious creamy and vegan alternative to the classic Christmas drink. Perfect to unwind with on Christmas Eve.

Ingredients:

1 15oz. can of full-fat coconut milk
6 medjool dates, pitted
¾ cup of raw cashews, soaked for 30 minutes
1 teaspoon of vanilla extract
3 tablespoons of spiced rum (optional)
1 teaspoon of freshly grated nutmeg
¼ teaspoon of xanthum gun (optional)
½ teaspoon of sea salt
2 cups of fresh water

Makes 14 servings.

Method:

1. Into a medium sized bowl place the cashews and then cover with boiling water and leave to soak for 30 minutes. When they are ready, drain and then rinse the cashews, placing them into a high-speed blender.

2. Add the fresh water into the blender with the cashews and blend for 2 minutes on a high setting.

3. Add the rest of the ingredients into the blender and blend for another two minutes until the dates are completely blended.

4. Stir the eggnog and serve into glasses and then garnish with some freshly grated nutmeg on top.

5. Enjoy the eggnog, chilled is best but it can be heated up and served warm too if preferred.

Starters

Warm Almond, Garlic and Parsnip Soup

This is a delicious dairy-free soup that is just as creamy – without any of the cream! A heart-warming bowl of soup to see you through the winter months and perfect as a Christmas starter.

Ingredients
300g parsnip
1 large yellow onion
1 tablespoon of olive oil
125g of almonds, blanched
1 garlic bulb (10 cloves)
1 tablespoon of apple cider vinegar or white wine
20 organic red grapes, divided with the seeds removed
4 cups of boiling water, or more to taste
2 sprigs of fresh thyme or 1tsp of dried thyme
Sea salt and freshly ground black pepper

Serves 4

Method

1. Preheat the oven to 200 degrees C or 400 degrees F. Prepare the vegetables by peeling the parsnip and then cutting it and the parsley, onion and the garlic into bite-sized pieces.

2. Place the vegetables into a bowl and drizzle lightly with olive oil, tossing to coat.
3. Place the vegetables into the oven and then bake for 15-20 minutes until they become lightly browned and tender.

4. In the meantime, blanch the almonds by heating them in hot water long enough to remove their skin. Drain. Once the vegetables are heated, remove them from the oven and place them into a heatproof blender.

5. Add in the hot water, blanched almonds, thyme, apple cider vinegar and the sea salt and black pepper for seasoning. Blend until the mixture is completely smooth.

6. Taste the mixture and adjust the flavors according to your preferences. Serve the soup immediately into bowls and then drizzle over some olive oil, thyme and the grapes for garnish.

This is a beautiful thick soup that will warm the cockles of your heart and is especially delicious when served with seeded granary bread.

Ingredients

4 or 5 cups of cauliflower florets
1½ cups of cashew cream
6 scallions, chopped roughly
2 shallots, chopped roughly
1 celery stalk, roughly chopped
2TB of vegan butter such as Earth Balance (or other non-dairy spread), divided
2-3 cups of vegetable broth

Serve with:
Sliced mushrooms
Freshly chopped parsley
Sea salt and black pepper

Serves 4

Method

1. Place 1 tablespoon of vegan butter into a heavy stock pan over a medium heat, along with the cauliflower florets and the water. Cover and soften for around 20 minutes, until the cauliflower has absorbed the water.

2. Place the cauliflower florets into a blender and leave to cool. Puree into a smooth mixture before adding the cashew cream and pureeing again.

3. Return to the stockpot and add in 1 tablespoon of vegan butter with the shallots, scallions and the celery. Sauté over a medium to high heat until thoroughly softened which will take about 4 minutes. Then transfer the mixture to the blender and leave it to cool slightly, before pureeing until smooth.

4. Add the contents of the blender into the stockpot and stir in the 2 cups of vegetable broth, adding more as necessary if you want the soup to be thinner.

5. Add the fresh parsley in with the sautéed mushrooms. Serve immediately.

This one takes a little preparation in terms of creating the almond cheese, but once it's ready, it can be stored in the fridge and eaten with your favorite breads or crackers.

Ingredients

145g ground almonds
3 tbsps olive oil
2 garlic cloves, minced
60ml lemon juice
½ cup of water (4 fl oz.)
1 ¼ tsp of sea salt
Dill (for garnish)
12 crostini (for serving)

Serves 4

Method

1. Into a blender place all of the above ingredients and then process until the mixture is smooth and super creamy which should only take a couple of minutes.

2. Take a small bowl and line with the three layers of cheesecloth. Carefully spoon the mixture into the cheesecloth and tie the sides of the cheesecloth together, so it forms a ball. Use a rubber band to keep it together and then place the ball within a strainer, over a bowl.

3. Place within the fridge for 12 hours and leave it to set. After 12 hours there should only be a little amount of liquid left and this can be drained off. If you're going to use the same dish, then you can wash the drained

liquid out. Give the dish a touch of cooking spray to ensure that it's easily removed.

4. Preheat the oven to 180 degrees and while unwrapping the cheese from out of the cloth, transfer into a greased baking dish. Alternatively you can transfer the cheese smooth side up into a linked baking sheet.

5. Bake in the oven for 40 minutes until the cheese is a golden brown color. It will appear cracked on the top and be firm to the touch.

6. Serve the almond feta cheese onto crostini with a drizzling of olive oil and dill if preferred.

This is a scrumptious starter to indulge in before a Christmas meal or Boxing Day Lunch.

Ingredients
3 ripe pears, quartered and cored – leave the peel on
100g pack of walnuts, broken into pieces
12 Medjool dates, chopped and de-stoned
225g bag of mixed salad leaves
1 large watercress, with sprigs divided
100g of soy yoghurt
300g of vegan cheese (Daiya or Violife for example)
Juice of 1 lime
1-2 tablespoon of ginger syrup
Walnut oil, for drizzling

Serves 6

Method

1. Slice the pears into quarters and then toss into a bowl along with the lime juice – this helps with protecting their natural color. To make the vegan cheese dressing, mix together the soy yoghurt with half of the vegan cheese, the ginger syrup and 3-4 tablespoons of water to create a smooth and thick coating.

2. Spread the pear slices onto the plates and top with the dates, walnuts and the remainder of the vegan cheese. This can be created around 1 hour before serving the salad.

3. Drizzle the salad with some of the walnut oil and the vegan cheese dressing. Season with black pepper. If you want more dressing, mix the watercress and the

salad leaves together and add more to each plate as necessary.

This is a healthy salad that's nutritious and delicious, as well as being easy to prepare.

Ingredients

4 large tomatoes, chopped into pieces
4 avocados, peeled, de-stoned and diced
1 red onion, sliced thinly
1 8 ounce bottle of balsamic vinaigrette
¼ teaspoon of ground black pepper

Serves 6

Method

1. Into a large serving bowl, combine the avocados, tomatoes and the red onion together.

2. Add the black pepper and the balsamic vinaigrette dressing into the salad and then cover and chill for an hour, so that the flavors can combine.

Main Courses

Vegetable Lentil Loaf

This is a hearty combination of vegetables and lentils that makes a tasty replacement for turkey or meat based dishes.

Ingredients

For the loaf:
1 cup of dry red lentils (either green or brown)
1 small onion, diced finely
1 carrot, finely diced or grated
1 celery stalk, diced finely
1 small red bell pepper, diced finely
3 garlic cloves, minced

¾ cup oats
½ cup of oat flour
2 ½ cups of water or vegetable broth
3 tablespoons of flaxseed meal
2 tablespoons olive oil
1 heaped teaspoon of dried thyme
½ heaped teaspoon of cumin
½ teaspoon of garlic and onion powder
1/4 -1/2 teaspoon of ground chipotle pepper, optional
1/3 cup of water

For the glaze:
3 tablespoons of organic ketchup
1 tablespoon of balsamic vinegar
1 tablespoon of pure maple syrup

Serves 8

Method

1. Rinse the lentils and then in a large pot, place the 2½ cups of water with the lentils. Boil and then reduce the heat and cover for 40 minutes, allowing to simmer. Stir occasionally. Once cool, remove the lid and leave. Do not drain, the lentils should be left to thicken after standing – around 15 minutes is enough.

2. Preheat the oven to 350 degrees. Combine the flaxseed meal with 1/3 of a cup of water into a small bowl. Set this aside for 10 minutes, then place inside the refrigerator. The flaxseed meal acts as a binder and when left to sit, will thicken well.

3. Into a pan, heat the oil and sauté the prepared vegetables: the onion, garlic, bell pepper, celery and the carrots for around 5 minutes. Take the spices and add them in, mixing well to incorporate before setting aside and leaving to cool.

4. Into a food processor or an immersion blender, blend about ¾ of the lentil mixture. The other option is to mash lentils using a fork or a potato masher.

5. Combine the sautéed vegetables into the lentils, oats, the oat flour and flax egg, mixing the ingredients well. Add some salt and pepper to season as necessary. Place the lentil mixture into a loaf pan that's lined with parchment paper – allow some to overlap the pan so that the loaf can be easily removed later. Ensure that the loaf is pressed down firmly along the edges of the pan.

6. Into a small bowl, prepare the glaze by first combining the ketchup, balsamic vinegar and maple syrup, mixing well. Use heaped tablespoons to make the glazing so you will have plenty of this sauce for the top of the loaf.

7. Spread the glazing over the top of the loaf and then bake for 45-50 minutes in the oven. Leave the loaf to cool slightly before slicing.

Cashew Nut Loaf with Sage and Onion Stuffing

This is an excellent alternative to roast turkey with all of the trimmings. For a richer variation you can substitute the water and yeast extract with red or white wine, or even soya milk – depending on your preferences.

Ingredients
30g/1oz of margarine
1 medium leek, chopped finely
2 sticks of celery, chopped finely
1 teaspoon of yeast extract
3 cups of ground cashew nuts
2 tablespoons of soya flour
2 tablespoons of herbs
3 cups/6oz of white bread crumbs
Sage and onion stuffing
Sea salt and black pepper (for seasoning)
1½ cups of hot water

Serves 2-4

Method

1. Into a large pan, melt the margarine and cook the leek and celery for a few minutes. Into a jug, mix the yeast extract along with the hot water, before adding this in with the leek and celery.

2. Stir in the cashew nuts, soya flour, breadcrumbs and the herbs, along with the salt and pepper into the pan. Mix this well and then leave to cool slightly as you grease the loaf tin with a little margarine.

3. Place half of the nut roast mixture inside the tin. Press it down well. Add in the sage and onion stuffing,

continuing to press down firmly. Then place the rest of the nut roast mixture into the dish.

4. Bake in the oven for 40 minutes at 180C/360F, then remove from the tin.

5. Serve into slices with your favorite roast vegetables, gravy and cranberry sauce.

This is a fantastic alternative to a roast dinner. It's best prepared the day before for best results – and to save yourself any stress on Christmas Day.

Ingredients
1 cup of diced onion
4-5 garlic cloves, minced
¾ cup of toasted walnuts
½ cup of diced celery
2 cups of chickpeas (save 1/3 cup)
1/3 cup of rolled oats
1 prepared pastry pie crust, thawed
1 tablespoon of freshly chopped thyme
1/3 cup of dried cranberries
2 teaspoons of ground sage
1-10oz packet of frozen chopped spinach
1 tablespoons of olive oil or water (for sautéing)
½ tablespoon of olive oil
1 teaspoon of tamari
2 teaspoons of tamari
2 tablespoons of freshly squeezed lemon juice
2 tablespoons of walnuts, chopped
¼ teaspoon of sea salt
1/8 teaspoon of freshly ground black pepper

Serves 8

Method

1. Into a pan add the onion, oil, garlic, celery, sea salt and black pepper over a medium-high heat. Cook for 9-10 minutes, stirring occasionally until the mixture is thoroughly softened and golden in color.

2. Into a food processor add the sautéed mixture, the chickpeas (apart from the reserved 1/3 cup), 2 teaspoons of tamari, lemon juice, sage and sea salt. Partially puree and then add in the oats and toasted walnuts, pulsing them briefly to break up the nuts.

3. Transfer the mixture to a bowl and add in the cranberries, spinach, thyme, parsley and the chickpeas.

4. Place the mixture into the pie shell and smooth over to distribute it evenly. Combine the oil and the 1 teaspoon of tamari together and brush over the top of the pie, before sprinkling on the walnuts.

5. Into a preheated oven at 400 degrees, bake the tart until golden in color on the top and around the edges. This should take about 30-45 minutes.

6. Cool the pie for 5-10 minutes and then serve with gravy and cranberry sauce.

Lentil, Mushroom and Spinach Roulade

This roulade has a beautiful texture and is the ideal roast for vegetarians or vegans who don't like fake meats.

Ingredients

1 x 400g tin brown lentils, washed and drained
6 large mushrooms, chopped into small pieces
2 cups of cooked spinach, roughly chopped
6-8 sundried tomato halves
4 garlic cloves, finely chopped
4 tablespoons of olive oil
¼ teaspoon of onion powder
2-3 tablespoon of tomato paste
¼ teaspoon of coriander seeds
1 teaspoon od hot curry powder (optional)
1/8 cup water
1 cup of vegan melting cheese (optional)
¾ cup of freshly roasted whole hazelnuts, finely chopped (optional)
A few sprigs of fresh rosemary (optional)
Vegan milk to brush on the pastry

Serves 2-4

Method

1. Into a large frying pan, fry the mushrooms and garlic together, mixing well. Let them sweat and after a few minutes, add in the tomato paste, curry powder (if using) and onion powder, mixing well. Add in the cooked lentils and stir.

2. Add the spinach into the mixture, along with the remaining ingredients, but leave any 'Extras' for later. Cover the pan and allow to simmer for 20 minutes until

the mixture is thick, rich and aromatic. Remove from the heat and leave to cool for 15 minutes.

3. Place the thawed pastry sheets onto a clean kitchen surface and ensuring it's floured, roll the pastry sheets together until they form one large sheet of approximately 10 by 7 inches.

4. Spoon the spinach and lentil mixture onto the pastry sheet. Make sure that it's lukewarm as you place the mixture onto each sheet. Flatten the mixture and then distribute it evenly with the back of a large spoon. Add the grated vegan cheese to the mixture if using, topping with roasted nuts. You might want to leave a few nuts for dusting the roulade sides at the end, if necessary.

5. Start rolling the mixture away from you until it reaches the end. This might require another pair of hands, so if necessary ask for help. Once the roulade has been created, wash and dry your hands before proceeding with the next step.

6. Take some vegan milk and brush it along the roulade, creating horizontal cuts along the surface of the dough at half-inch intervals. These are markers to indicate where each slice is once cooked.

7. Preheat the oven to 400 degrees F/200C. Line an ovenproof dish with some grease proof paper, greasing it with a little margarine. Lift the roulade using 2 spatulas and carefully place inside of the tin.

8. Place the roulade into the hot oven for 20 minutes until it turns golden. Take out and then place the vegetables or plain new potatoes into a dish before serving.

Chestnut Stuffing & Mushroom Quinoa Roast

This is a luxurious nut roast that is packed full of exotic flavor, texture and aroma. Try it for yourself and you'll see how wonderful it tastes.

Ingredients

Nut Roast Base

For a 9" x 5" base tin

500g mushrooms, chopped
250g mushrooms, sliced
50g pine nuts
50g pistachio
1 cup/185g of quinoa, soaked overnight
1¼ cups of almond flour
1 serving of vegan egg replacer such as Orgran No Egg Replacer
50ml madeira (white wine)
1 teaspoon of fresh thyme leaves or 1½ teaspoons of dried thyme leaves
1 handful of fresh parsley, finely chopped
Vegan margarine, for frying
Lemon juice, for squeezing
2 pinches of salt

Stuffing

200g chestnuts
2 medium onions
125g of almonds
40-50g of vegan margarine
1 cup of ground almonds
8 large sage leaves, finely chopped
Salt and pepper to taste

Serves 4

Method

1. Chop the apricots and chestnuts into 1cm x 1cm pieces –
but don't make them too small.

2. Chop the onions then fry in the vegan margarine for couple
of minutes. Add in the chestnuts, apricots and the sage and
continue cooking for another 5 minutes. Add in the salt and
pepper to season as necessary.

3. Take the chestnut and apricot mixture from off the heat
   and then add in the ground almonds.

4. Roll the chestnut mixture into balls and place in the
   oven for 20 minutes at 150C to bake until golden brown
   in color. This stuffing mixture can also be used to
   create the topping for the nut roast.

5. For the nut roast fry the onions with the vegan
   margarine over a medium heat until the onions are soft.
   Add in the thyme and grated mushrooms and sauté for
   10 minutes longer. During this process the mushrooms
   may break down and become moist so remember to
   keep stirring.

6. Drain the quinoa and then rinse before draining again.
   Add the quinoa along with the madeira or the wine to
   the mixture. Place the lid on and allow the quinoa to
   steam for 8-10 minutes before stirring every 3 minutes.

7. Once the quinoa is just cooked, take off the lid and
   allow any excess moisture to disappear. In the
   meantime, place the pistachio and pine nuts onto a

baking tray and place in the oven at 170C to allow to toast. Keep an eye on them in case they burn!

8. Remove the nuts from the oven and placing them in a plastic bag, bash using a rolling pin to ensure they are broken up. Fry the mushrooms in another pan with more vegan margarine if needed. Once the mushroom mixture is cooked and dried off (which may take 30 minutes or so), add in the pine nuts and the pistachios.

9. Stir in the almond flour, parsley, fried mushrooms and the lemon juice into the pan, adding sea salt to taste. This mixture will be dry and yet rather sticky. You can add a vegan alternative to eggs such as Orgran No Egg Replacer if necessary as this will bind with the mixture and make the nut roast easier to slice once ready.

10. Take a 9" x 5" loaf pan and line it with baking paper. Place 2 rectangular pieces over the middle of the pan and cover both of the sides. Press the stuffing mixture firmly into the pan – it should be 1 and a 1/2-2cm thick. If you have any leftovers they can be made into stuffing balls.

11. Pour the nut roast mixture into the loaf tin and then press firmly down again. Place into the oven and bake at 170C for 11/2 hours until the nut roast is firm to touch.

12. Leave to cool for 5 minutes then cover with a plate. You will need to flip the pan over to turn the nut roast out. Allow to rest for 5 minutes longer before slicing.

Side Dishes

Roasted Brussels Sprouts with Cranberries and Pecans

This side dish is excellent when served with a nut roast, complimenting the flavors well.

Ingredients

1 pound of Brussels sprouts, trimmed and halved lengthwise
½ cup dried cranberries
¼ cup pecans, chopped
1/8 teaspoon granulated garlic
2 tablespoons extra virgin olive oil
¼ teaspoon cracked black pepper
½ teaspoon sea salt

Serves 4

Method

1. Preheat the oven to 400 degrees Fahrenheit. Into a large bowl, toss together the Brussels sprouts, extra-virgin olive oil, granulated garlic along with the sea salt and black pepper.

2. Onto a rimmed baking sheet, roast the mixture for around 30-35 minutes, stirring occasionally. Ensure that the roast Brussels sprouts are golden brown and crispy, yet tender inside before serving.

3. In the last 5-7 minutes of cooking, stir in the pecans and cranberries, before serving immediately.

Roast Potatoes, Parsnips and Carrots

Roast potatoes make an excellent addition to any roast dinner, while the carrots and parsnips are a firm favorite that can add a roasted flavor to any festive meal.

Ingredients

1.2kg potatoes
6 carrots
6 parsnips
1 garlic bulb
3 sprigs of fresh rosemary
Olive oil
Sea salt
Freshly ground black pepper

Serves 6

Method

1. If you want to cook the vegetables on their own, then preheat the oven to 200 degrees C/400 degrees F/gas mark 6. Peel the vegetables first and then halve them lengthways. Tear the garlic bulb into cloves and with them unpeeled, bash them with the palm of your hand slightly. Pick the rosemary leaves away from their woody stalks.

2. Place the potatoes into the large pan, along with the carrots. Add boiling water and bring to the boil for 5 minutes before adding parsnips and then cooking for 4 minutes longer.

3. Drain the potatoes in a colander and then leave to steam dry. Remove the carrots and the parsnips, placing them to one side. Using the colander, fluff up the potatoes, shaking them a little so they are crisp when cooked.

4. Add a few tablespoons of olive oil into a large roasting tray, along with the garlic and the rosemary leaves. Place the vegetables into the roasting tray, along with a pinch of sea salt and black pepper, stirring to coat the vegetables.

5. Coat the vegetables with the seasoning to flavor, then place them into the preheated oven for 1 hour until they are crisp and golden. Serve with your favorite festive vegan main course.

Steamed Leeks with Mustard and Shallot Vinaigrette

This is a rich and flavorsome side dish that's excellent when served alongside roast potatoes and vegetables.

Ingredients

2 large leeks cut into 2 ½ inch strips
1 small shallot, minced
1 teaspoon of balsamic vinegar
1 tablespoon red wine vinegar
¼ cup of extra virgin olive oil
1 tablespoon Dijon mustard
1 tablespoon chopped parsley
Sea salt and freshly ground black pepper

Serves 4

Method

1. In a saucepan with a steamer basket and 1 inch of water, bring to the boil. Add in the leeks and then cover and steam for about 5 minutes until tender. Drain the leeks and then pat them dry. Then refrigerate until chilled which should take about 10 minutes.

2. Into a small bowl, add the shallot and the mustard and combine with the balsamic and the red wine vinegars, whisking in the olive oil and salt and black pepper for seasoning.

3. Place the steamed leeks onto plates and then drizzle with the vinaigrette, sprinkling with the parsley before serving.

This mixture of kale and potatoes goes together surprisingly well, especially with a lentil roast smothered in cranberry sauce or mushroom gravy.

Ingredients

For the potatoes:
5 large potatoes, peeled and chopped
2 cloves of garlic, peeled and smashed
2 tablespoons vegan margarine (such as Earth Balance), at room temperature
1 teaspoon of kosher salt

For the kale:
3 tablespoons of extra-virgin olive oil
1 small onion, diced
2 cloves of garlic
One 12 ounce bunch of kale, stemmed and chopped into 1 inch pieces
½ teaspoon of kosher salt
¼ cup of low-sodium vegetable broth

Method

1. Add the potatoes, garlic, sea salt and margarine into a saucepan along with cold water. Cover. Bring this mixture to the boil and leave over a medium-high heat. Then reduce the heat to a simmer and cook until the potatoes are tenderized – in about 15-20 minutes.

2. Drain the potatoes and remove the garlic cloves from the colander. Return the potatoes to the pan and mash with a potato masher.

3. To prepare the kale, heat some oil into a large skillet and place over a medium-high heat. Add in the onion, sea salt and black pepper, cooking until translucent which takes about 6 minutes. Add in the garlic for an aromatic flavor which takes about 30 seconds. Add the kale and the vegetable broth together, stirring during the cooking process until the kale is wilted which should take 10-12 minutes.

4. Assemble the kale mixture together along with the vegetable broth, margarine, sea salt and black pepper to the potatoes. Place over a low heat and warm through until smooth, before seasoning with salt and pepper. Transfer the mixture into a bowl and then serve.

This pilaf dish is healthy, hearty and wholesome and along with being colorful, is a great side dish to serve with a vegan roast.

Ingredients

1 cup quinoa, rinsed in a sieve
1 medium yellow or red onion, finely chopped
1 small head cauliflower, cut into pieces and florets
2 cups of low-sodium vegetable broth
1/3 cup of toasted pine nuts
½ cup dried cranberries
¼ cup fresh parsley, to taste
1 tablespoon of olive oil
1 tablespoon of walnut or sesame seed oil
Sea salt
Freshly ground black pepper

Serves 6

Method

1. Add the quinoa and the broth into a saucepan and then bring to a slow boil. Cover then simmer for 15 minutes until the water is thoroughly absorbed.

2. Heat the oil in a frying pan or skillet. Add in the onion, sautéing on a medium-low heat until the mixture is golden. Add the cauliflower in and 1/3 of a cup of water. Cover the pan and cook for 5 minutes until the cauliflower becomes tender.

3. After the quinoa has cooked, add it in with the cauliflower mixture, along with the parsley, cranberries,

the walnut or sesame seed oil if using and the lemon juice. Combine all of these ingredients together and then remove from the heat. Cover the pan and then cook for another 5 minutes until the cauliflower becomes tenderized.

Sauces

Mushroom Gravy

This thick and meat-like gravy tastes delicious with plenty of mashed potato and goes especially well with seitan based roasts.

Ingredients

8 ounces of mushrooms (porcini, cremini or shiitake)
1 cup chopped white onion
4 garlic cloves, finely chopped
2 ¼ cups of low sodium vegetable broth, divided
¼ cup of Merlot of other spicy red wine
2 tablespoons finely chopped fresh thyme
1 tablespoon finely chopped fresh rosemary
2 tablespoons reduced-sodium tamari
2 tablespoons cornstarch
2 tablespoons nutritional yeast

¼ teaspoon of ground black pepper

Makes approximately 3 cups

Method

1. Into a large skillet, add the onion and cook over a medium-high heat for 3-4 minutes until it becomes translucent. Add about ¼ cup of vegetable broth into the pan so as to prevent the onion from burning at the bottom. Add in the mushrooms, cooking for 10-12 minutes until they begin to release their liquid.

2. Stir in the rosemary, garlic and thyme, cooking continuously for 1 minute until the mushrooms are fragrant. Add wine into the mixture and cook for 1 minute further, stirring frequently. Add in the remaining 2 cups of broth and then bring to a simmer.

3. Into a small bowl, whisk together the cornstarch, yeast and tamari until a thick paste is formed. Add the mixture into the skillet and whisk throughout until the paste dissolves completely. Bring to the mixture to the boil, cooking for 1 minute and stirring all the time. Add pepper as needed and then serve the gravy hot.

This rich and satisfying gravy tastes excellent when poured over a succulent nut roast and served with potatoes and vegetables.

Ingredients

1 tablespoon of olive oil
1 large onion, thinly sliced
300ml of vegetable stock
100ml of white wine
1 tablespoon of plain flour
1 ½ teaspoons sugar

Serves 4

Method

1. Into a large frying pan, heat the olive oil. Add in the onion and sprinkle with the teaspoon and a half of sugar.

2. Sprinkle some of the flour over the onion, stirring and cooking for a minute. Stir in the stock and the wine gradually before bringing to the boil and then reducing the heat and leaving to simmer gently until thickened.

Tangerine Cranberry Sauce

This sweet serving sauce adds a zesty tang to vegetables – as well as being healthy!

Ingredients

4 tangerines or clementines, washed well
12 ounces of fresh cranberries
2 cups of fresh orange juice
1 cup of sugar

Makes 4 cups

Method

1. Cut the tangerines into ½ inch slices by cutting them crosswise through the skins. Quarter the slices. Into a small bowl toss in the tangerines along with ½ a cup of the sugar. Cover and then keep in the fridge overnight.

2. Into a heavy and medium sized saucepan, combine the tangerines and their liquid, along with the ½ cup of sugar and the 2 cups of orange juice. Bring the mixture to the boil, simmer over a low heat until the tangerine skins soften and the liquid becomes syrupy which should take about 50 minutes.

3. Add the cranberries into the same pan with the tangerines, cooking over a medium-low heat until the skins soften and split which takes around 15 minutes.

4. Drain both the tangerines and the cranberries in the colander and then set over a bowl, before returning the liquid to the saucepan. Allow the liquid to boil over a moderate high heat until it becomes syrupy, in about 15

minutes. Pour the syrup over the fruit and then leave to cool completely before serving.

Apple and Cranberry Chutney

This sweet and hearty chutney is the perfect condiment to serve with your favorite vegan or cashew nut cheese and crackers.

Ingredients
500g eating apples, peeled and chopped into large chunks
1kg of cooking apples, peeled and chopped into small chunks
50g fresh root ginger, finely chopped
450g onions, sliced
500g granulated sugar
250ml cider vinegar
500g cranberries
1 teaspoon of peppercorns

Makes 4 medium sized jars

Method

1. Add all of the ingredients into a large saucepan, except for the cranberries. Gently heat and stir until the sugar is dissolved completely. Bring the mixture to the boil, reduce the heat and simmer for 50 minutes, uncovered. Stir regularly until the apples and onions are tenderized and the mixture is thick with no watery or juicy remains.

2. Add the cranberries into the mixture and cook for 10 minutes further until the fruit is softened, but not burst.

3. Spoon the hot chutney into clean jars and then seal. Store the jar unopened in a dark and cool place. This chutney can keep for around 6 months and it's advised to chill upon opening.

This bread sauce recipe is wonderful for dipping roast potatoes into, or served with your favorite roasted vegetables.

Ingredients
1 large onion, peeled
1 teacup of fresh white breadcrumbs
6-8 garlic cloves
½ pint soya milk
Vegan margarine
Vegan cream (optional)

Makes approximately 2 servings

Method

1. Place the garlic cloves and the onion into a saucepan along with the soya milk. Heat the mixture until it starts boiling then remove from the heat and leave it to infuse for an hour or so.

2. Add in a large knob of vegan margarine, the breadcrumbs and the salt and pepper. Combine the mixture well and then cook on a low heat for around 15 minutes.

3. Before serving, remove the onion from the sauce and add a little vegan cream if necessary.

Desserts

Christmas Brandy Truffles

These decadent truffles are a delight to behold upon the dinner table and are perfect when served with coffee.

Ingredients

450g/1lb icing sugar
345g/12oz dark chocolate
1 tub vegan 'cream cheese' such as Tofutti
Dark cocoa powder
1 tablespoon of dried cranberries
1½ teaspoon of brandy
200g/7oz icing sugar (for the topping)
1 tub green angelica, cut into leaf shapes

Makes about 25 truffles

Method:

1. In a bowl, add the vegan cream cheese, sieving in the icing sugar and beating the mixture well until smooth.

2. Break the dark chocolate into small pieces in a bowl, immersing it into a saucepan and then simmering in the water. Stir the mixture with a wooden spoon until it's thoroughly melted.

3. Add the melted chocolate and the vegan cheese to the icing mixture. Add in the brandy. Mix well and then cover and place in the refrigerator for 1 hour.

4. Remove the mixture from the fridge and shape into truffles of approximately ½ inch balls. Place the cocoa

powder in a bowl, dip the truffles in and shake gently until they are thoroughly coated.

5. Combine the icing sugar and the water together. Spoon this onto the truffles and then garnish each with the cranberries and angelica leaves. Store in a container until ready and then place on your favorite serving dish.

Gluten-Free Pecan Pie

This pecan pie recipe is an excellent alternative to Christmas cake.

Ingredients
½ cup of raw pecans
4 cups of Almond meal
1 cup of raisins
2/3 cup of pure maple syrup
2/3 cup coconut milk, canned
1 cup of cinnamon
Extra pecans to garnish

Serves 6

Method

1. Place the maple syrup and the almond meal into a large bowl, mixing well until sticky. Remove the mixture and then transfer to a 9" pie tin. Using a spatula, press the mixture into the bottom and the sides of the pie, ensuring it's even. Set it aside.

2. Add the pecans into the food processor, mixing until there are no big chunks left. Add in the coconut milk, then blend again with the raisins and the cinnamon. Continue blending until smooth.

3. Take the filling out of the food processor and then pour the mixture into the piecrust. Take a spatula and smooth and even out the mixture.

4. Garnish with the pecans and then chill inside the refrigerator so the pecan pie sets for an hour. The pie can be served as it is, or can be frozen and brought out later.

This vegan version of the classic mince pie recipe has all of the flavor without any of the animal products. You will need a round pastry cutter and enough bun tins to cook 30 pies.

Ingredients

Pastry
8oz soya margarine
8oz icing sugar
1lb plain flour

Mincemeat
6 oz mixed dried fruit
3 oz bramley apples, cored and chopped small
2 oz soft dark brown sugar
1 oz vegetarian suet
1 teaspoon of mixed ground spice
1 pinch of ground cinnamon
1 pinch of fresh grated nutmeg
A small handful of almonds, chopped
1 tablespoon of brandy

Juice and grated zest of half an orange or lemon

Method

To make the pastry:

1. Sift the icing sugar and the flour together into a mixing bowl. Add the margarine in with the flour and rub together quickly using your fingertips so that it becomes like fine breadcrumbs in terms of consistency. Make sure there are no large margarine lumps remaining.

2. Bring together the mixture so that it forms a dough, then add water, a teaspoon at a time. Add some more flour if it becomes too wet.

To make the mincemeat:

1. Place all of the mincemeat ingredients into the saucepan and on a low heat cook the mixture, stirring everything frequently until soft.

2. Remove from the heat and allow the pan to cool. Stir occasionally.

3. Once the mixture is cold, stir thoroughly again.

To make the mince pie:

1. Roll the pastry out to 3mm thickness. Cut out a large circle for the base and then a smaller circle – this will be the lid.

2. Put the base in the bun tin and then fill with the mincemeat. Put the lid on the top and pinch the edges so that it joins with the base.

3. Repeat the process until all of the pastry and the mincemeat is gone. Any leftover pastry can be used to decorate pies with.

4. Preheat the oven to 200 degrees C or gas mark 6. If using a fan oven, set it to around 180 degrees C.

5. Place the mince pies in the oven for about 20 minutes – they will be golden in color when ready to remove.

6. Remove the mince pies from the oven. Take the pies from the tin and then leave to cool for 5 minutes on a wire cooling rack. Dust the mince pies with icing sugar before serving.

This is a rich and festive fruit cake that's actually fairly healthy, being low fat and also containing no processed sugar.

Ingredients

3 oz/85g mixed nuts, roughly chopped
4 oz/115g chopped dried apricots
12 oz/340g mixed dried fruit
3 oz/85g plain wholemeal flour
3 oz/85g plain white flour
8 oz/250g dates
8 fl oz/240ml water
2 teaspoon of baking powder
1 teaspoon of mixed spice
4 tablespoon of orange juice
4 tablespoons of rum

Serves 6-8

Method

1. Preheat the oven to 170 degrees/340 F/gas mark 4.

2. Place both the dates and the water into a saucepan and bring it to the boil. Cook for five minutes gently, until the dates are soft. Mash them using a fork and then add the rest of the ingredients, mixing well.

3. Spoon the cake mixture into a lined 2lb/900g cake tin, smoothing the top. Bake for 1.5 hours.

4. For an alternate option, add half of the cake mixture into the tin, followed by a layer of marzipan and then another layer of cake. The other option is to add the marzipan onto the top layer, followed by the white icing.

5. Store in a cool place. The cake can be stored for around a week.

This delicious fudge makes for a great snack and a unique Christmas presented when presented in a gift jar.

Ingredients

1 cup of vegan white or dark chocolate (rice milk chocolate for example)
½ cup of coconut cream concentrate (coconut butter)
1 teaspoon of vanilla extract
¾ teaspoon of liquid peppermint stevia
¼ teaspoon of sea salt (optional)
Crushed peppermint candies (optional, for garnishing)

Makes approximately 10 pieces of fudge

Method

1. Into a double boiler, melt the chocolate and the coconut cream concentrate together over a medium heat. Stir throughout.

2. Taking a mold, line the sides and the bottom with plastic wrap, so that there is enough room for 'handles' during the unmolding process.

3. Once most of the mixture has melted, reduce the temperature to a low heat and add in the peppermint stevia and the sea salt, mixing well.

4. Pour the mixture into the mold, being careful as you do so to gently tap the sides to ensure a flat surface.

5. Sprinkle some crushed peppermint candies on the top of the fudge, pressing lightly into the fudge. Allow the mixture to cool in the fridge for 1 hour.

6. Take the fudge out of the fridge and remove the container, allowing it to come to room temperature. This takes about 5 minutes.

7. On a cutting board, press down on the fudge using a serrated knife and cut the fudge into appropriate sized pieces. Place the fudge in a covered container and store in the fridge.

Thank you for reading this recipe book. I hope you enjoyed it and found some tasty Christmas vegan recipes to try out!

If you liked this book I would appreciate if you could leave me an Amazon review, as that greatly helps out self-published authors like me. Thank you!

Please visit this link to leave a review:

http://www.amazon.com/dp/B00QMNP4V4

13809084R00036

Printed in Great Britain
by Amazon